the upwards we could still climb

Upwards Spiraling Poetry from

Luke Maguire Armstrong

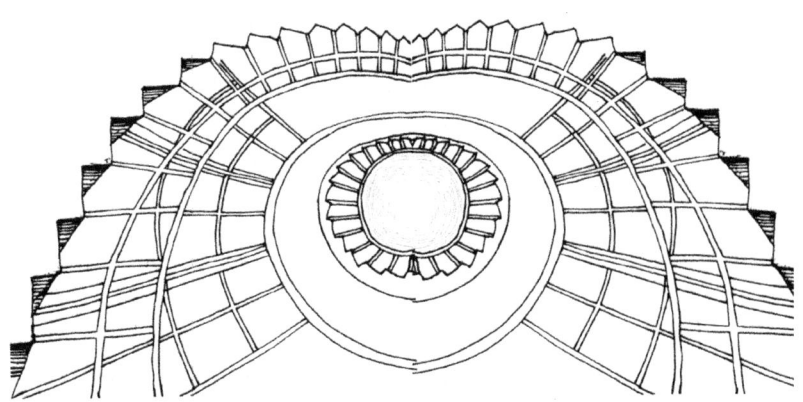

Copyright © 2022 Luke Maguire Armstrong

All Rights Reserved.

From Paññā Press
IG: @PannaPress
From @KarunaAtitlan

Reserved for what and who? Reserved specially for you to meander through. May our hearts join in this poetic outpouring welling from my heart. I reserve the right to allow you to do with these poems as you wish. Post them if you feel the call, tattoo them on your bum—whatever, it's our world and I'm happy to be here with you in it.

Squirrel.

ISBN: 9798820413391

Cover design and interior layout by the author.

Image on page 8 from Baron Ejförd. Legend.

Yummy, ice cream!

the upwards we could still climb

What mountain to climb?
What stretch of path shimmers in the distance?
Who will I be then?
Who am I now?
Who will I be if I don't embark?
Always these questions,
Yet it's not their answers I seek,
but the journey of them,
the way they weave
to me and through me on their pilgrimage within me.
I walk
with these companions,
compasses,
guides,
gilded by what galvanizes a
poet's heart to pour out with words
what cannot be
put into form
in this shapeless space
that forges us.

TEA TABLE OF CONTENTS

      Authors Note   i

1 Patience

3 Cruelty

5 This Whirling Twirling

9 A Secret You Know

12 The Indulgence of Our Wildest Imaginings

16 Dear Sojourners

17 A Lot

18 Beloved Ineffable Things

20 I Cling

22 Imagine

23 When I See You

25 This

27 Let us Speculate

28 A Close Encounter with a notebook

the upwards we could still climb
30 Life is Living
36 Poetry Manifesto
48 Permission to
    Take this Book
    from a Store

Author's Note

Persistent, the moonlight. Contrary to the precedent set by my previous collections, I'm writing my author's note early on in the process of compiling and refining this tome. There are still a lot of pieces to put together and ironing out to do—but I can feel it emerging—something being belonging to a future book is flowing out of me.

Right now, it's 5:10am—I've been up since the 3am hour—no alarm clock—the moonlight woke me again and brought me to this manuscript. "Help me come to be," it whispers to me in a voice deeper than anything I know. Soon it will be Christmas.

Now it's the New Year and again I'm up at some limbo hour of the morning adding to this note and book. If you're looking for poetry, I suggest you search for it in an inhale beneath the stars, exhaling exalted delight, a voyager passing through the night.

The early morning is an eternal urge. The willingness we find within to craft beauty is another name for The Way, that great passage that is our life.

Thanks to the early morning owl for her chanted question "Who?" Thank you, dearest reader, partaker of this communion through words, I bow to you. I celebrate us. I dance in delight at the way we've found each other amid all the scenarios that could have kept us apart.

Together for the human revolution,
—Luke

*Dedicated to you dear reader.
Your support makes my heart sing.*

Patience

Patience is a humbleness held out to the future,
a softening into accepting how finite we are
and what futility we face
if we hold tight to the hounds of control,
as if we could demand of life
and she would sway to the whims
of our ways.

In this world,
live within your body.
In this body,
live within our world.
Life is slow and unfathamable,
like forgiveness,
yet contemplateable,
like all you love and enjoy,
is that way of happily waiting.
It's deep and wide, and
on sunny days
you can float on upon it,
breathing in deep until
your belly is buoyant.
Let the sun melt your
worries and fears away.
On cool nights leave
the digital deserts to
lie awake and see the stars shiver

from the cold dark they burn within.

Why not?—give up the ever-amassing plans
and live a life wide and open?
Like a barn in spring,
the animals frisky,
they hold no ceremonies but rest
in the mystic gladness that through
our rituals we try to touch.

All you need to do is
open the door to the daylight
and wait for peace to settle in
like an afternoon breeze
carrying each inhale,
combined aromas,
a culinary art,
shaping
line draped linens
like haphazard
destinies
authored by wind.

I belong
to a beating heart,
palpitations in the places
I've paced around,
touching the earth of all life
looking for a place where to
set down the burdens of a lifetime
to be held while holding
it all.

Cruelty

Comes like an arrow that shatters porcelain cups set
on the table of my heart.
Antiques, rare finds, delicate shapes, shattered by
the something
I can't quite comprehend.
Who is this terror?
Yet how dark must their nights?
How unbearable those undistracted moments alone
to face the mind like a mirror reflecting the sun.

And within this contemplation
I feel the flow of compassion.
Not pity.
Not acceptance.
Not allowing.
But making allowance for their mistake,
they confused kindness with weakness.

But I am not some willow
who weeps in harsh winds.
Though I touch the finest of porcelain things,
I remain as fierce as the fire
that forms the glass.
But I will not burn you.

I am like the eagle looking
for the highest height.

From my sublime soaring
I see how cruelty is just another way of shrinking,
a cornered soul growling to
hide the whimpers.

So I will hold this wish for you,
that you find the wings and see
this world from your own soaring heights,
that you will use your own fire
to forge the finest things
instead of setting the world around you aflame.

Cruelty, I offer you my hope,
that you find your
way through your caverns and cool your fires.
Only you can.
My strength is in my every inch of hoping
for your happiness.
Forgiveness is but another way we keep the heart
warm and open to the frozen winds that blow
across the rock-hard fields of winter.

patience is a humbleness held out to the future

This Whirling Twirling

This great symmetry within it all—
repeating forms of shell and coral,
and the shapes of the cycles
we circle within.

We are strange loops,
dervishes in a twirling cosmos.
Who dares to spin from the center?
—itself a pattern found from conch shells
to that great center
galaxies spiral around.

Have you searched the vast fields of empty space?
Have you carried yourself quietly across the deserts
you deserted yourself within?

Here on earth we have errant atoms and bus stops
and smiling and stupas where elder women bow;
and there is calculating and grandfathers who call
the ground, "Friend," who leave offerings
just the way their grandmother did.
And there are cold souls and the icy blades of
separation and there is speculation and selfishness
that leaves children to raise themselves.
May they raise themselves as high
as the world sinks low.

And there are reunions

and well-employed regrets
and social benefit concerts
and mother squirrels suckling
suckling
suckling
their young.

So why not be hopeful?
Who are you but some blessed child of life herself?
Remember those baby, suckling, suckling, suckling
squirrels
with their soft closed eyes
the next time you feel like dropping all you love
into the cold winds of despair and regret.
You are being fed like this too,
but you're so young,
eyes so closed, you cannot see it.
But within the warmth of your body,
maybe you can feel it.
Hold yourself
to feel the warmth of something living,
living,
living,
something in you keeps you
from the cold all around.

No one cares or can control it,
you can decorate the inner sanctum
of your mind as you please.
I try to fill mine with soft, warm things.
I dwell with the flowers
then return to the earth with new seeds.

I like to keep music and incense about the room —
delicate treasures,
but not all will survive
the earthquakes
that rumble on
outside.

There will also be storms.
And times with no one steering and nowhere to go.
There will be times of no looking back and times
when all you can do is look behind and waiver.
You see, our world is
so saturated with living,
it is also filled
with dying.

That's the biggest one you'll face.
And in between there is waiting
and wondering
and times when your hands are full of seeds
when what your earth really needs is a good
weeding.

The only way to soften hardening ground
is to cast your song.
You shape your song
even in the shadows.
So see them kindly when
shadows look at you
with no love in their eyes.

Sing to silence and she will listen.

Say to silence what will beckon you
into her folds.
It's only paltry, poetry,
if you don't reach into you
to touch the place it reaches from.

It's only when you've nothing left to lose
that you stand to gain what you can not lose
and it's only after you've lost everything
that you'll find
what that is.

A Secret You Know

I will tell you a secret you already know,
whispered from that place
where all things grow.

Linger, laugher,
on our lips.
Love this way of waiting,
with palms open.
Everyday find a million ways
to light up a grin.

When love left her home
and set out for the
pure land,
she left so much behind —
the heavy tools that built
a thousand yesterdays,
into towers of sand.
She left the vain hopes
stacked before
the future.
One day, we all go dim,
but there is hope
in every smile.

I'm not afraid anymore,
to retrace all the steps,
to hold your hand and take each

step like chocolate coins
hidden in the Easter fields
of your youth.

I call you as you,
but I don't know
if you are in this world
or the memory of a possibility
that pulsed when I looked up
at the sky and dropped my
last doubt like a leaf into the wind.

Warm is the willingness to
slow the wheel of worry.
Happy is the impulse to hasten our pace
on the path that pervades us.
Worthy is the wisdom that
knows the difference.

So whatever comes,
what matter
if you are allied to
the unshakable ground beneath you?

Why not cast our joy to the sorrowing
and lend our strength to the weak?
Why not leave
every tired little plan
involving anything
other than that utmost
surrender to the ever ascending path
you climb within.

This old habit,
Running like a rabbit
through the hills of mind

The Indulgence of Our Wildest Imaginings

There is a strange pulse
to all things,
an ascending symmetry
born within the pieces of
the places pondered
in time, where
delight dances
within everything
beyond it all.

No one is guilty.
Many misguided,
miscalculating,
misadventuring,
venturing into places
we'd rather not know.
"Rejoice," she said,
"at each regret."
Each shows a way you
strangle and strand
your heart.

So many seeds in me,
So many mees I could be.
But only one in the end

to befriend:
the best of me.

I tore myself into a thousand little pieces
I threw into the wind and watched how
in time everything settles
and washes away.
Each regret of every yesterday,
has taught you
how to say, "Okay" to the unerring instinct that in
spite of hurricanes, the wind is our friend.

Forgiveness is the
great calm
at the center of every storm.
Be someone who re-writes the world into a story
that restores it.
Walk softly.
Speak gently.
Listen kindly.

You've heard the sufis knocking
on the inner door. You've sat and searched the lotus
of midnight, sitting for days watching how
everything rises
and falls away.

There's is a lighthouse in my sleep.
A wish on my pillow.
A light way I caress the
storm called mind.
This temple in the tempest,

a song of minstrels sent at dawn
singing of night
swaying and shaking
to the rhythms of unseen things.

Once I drowned a broken heart
in an ocean of trust.
I watched a thousand what ifs bow
gracefully to what was.
If you smile at the world,
it smiles back.
If you learn to fall in love with letting go, then love
will fill your life even in those moments
when it feels like it's taking all you love away.

No matter what we do during the morning, we'll
have to meet the afternoon sooner or later, when the
day is drab and the plans uncertain, that space on
the other side of serenity where sirens
whirl in distant alleyways,
just close enough to enter your life, just far enough
to be removed from it, the legend of Kali,
stalking from the places
we fear might be.

But always somewhere is a song, and ever heroic
deeds being done. Like a monument to expired
moments, we remember the reverence life showed
in the face of our follies and the allowance and
indulgence of our wildest imaginings and how
everything settles,
then washes away.

Everything settled
and washed away.

The things you love come and go,
so do not cling to the sands
of their shores.
Soak in the sun.
Swim in the surf.
Dance within
the moment,
trip between laughter and glee.
I do not know to where I'll go,
just that the jolly folly of life has led me by her
restless hands and wherever this is, wherever I am,
however life goes and dies,
it is happening and
we are within it,
settling and
walking our way
on a tidal path
that washes away.

Dear Sojourners

Dear sojourner searching for light in this life,
if there's anything I've learned
it's do not worry.
If there's anything I've uncovered it's that
a true smile doesn't hide from what hurts.

What is happening to the humans?
What has happened to the humans
that makes them live like this?

In San Francisco you can walk
through the bottom rungs and
see human hands
still holding on,
educated addicts who
for want of a feeling
give everything away.
If you manage to catch
that deep look pacing behind their eyes
you'll see it's
a window
through which you can understand
why our world hasn't found a harbor
within which there are no forgotten hearts.

A Lot

We're all facing a lot
descendants of krill
asking after their soul.
We're all faced with that
insatiable certainty.

Who are these people
And buildings
And views
And reds
And blues
And whites
And skirts
And the places that
Could yet be and the
People we might yet become.

Find the voice of your
Subtle pulse within—
here is a life taking it all in,
this fervent hope,
the lingering of longing
to lift you to the heights
of dreams on your darkest midnight.

The memory of tomorrow feels like a promise
that together we rose and remembered
the reason we came to be.

Beloved Ineffable Things

There is a light that shines at dawn
that is the sunrise.
Every single day everywhere on earth,
happening always somewhere,
the night is transformed into the day.
Have you ever known a teacher
with such an obvious and ever-unfolding lesson?
And each day we can do it too — the only hope
worthy of casting
into tomorrow is the hope that we will shine
as bright as we do today.
Whisper "how bright" into the air and watch how
thoroughly you can wink at
your shadows and move past them.
Shadows, just byproducts of the light.

We are what we always dreamed we might become
and within that is a vast dawning
of opportunity to deepen
into the feeling of rising to the occasion written
in every ounce of what we know
and the ineffable certainty hiding behind it all.

Things blossom
in their own time.
There's always some tether,
that holding on, a holding in,

that holding back,
and the awareness of how tightly you hold
is an early sign that you are letting it go.

Dear pilgrims of the unlikely path,
thank you for your light.
Thank you for the way you kept it burning alive
in yourself when all the forces around you plotted
to blow it out.
Thank you for being the inevitable being you are.
Whatever hidden arrangement of forces have
crystallized into your existing, I bet they do this sort
of stuff all the time. Why do you think they need so
many galaxies to play within?

So I say, throw away your clocks and rip down your
calendars. But I say it from an iPhone, which is both
a clock and a calendar.

1 Cling

Grasping, aversion,
Anger, avarice, illusion—
What fear of these storms?
What fear while clinging to rock?
Here is a petrichor paradise,
So thrust your hands through the soil
vegetation, lie on this loam and dig dig dig,
You will know you have dug far enough with you
cling to Dharma,
surrender to Allah,
die in Christ—
and be unable to discern any difference.

Don't wait for others,
not while everyone
mourns and moans
and cries and cripples the same way.
We elate and relate and copulate
and jubilate and terminate
after our epic arcs resolve
their heights, like life
moves forward from a permanent
resting place held in the
fields of our heart.

We all long to live
but all lose and die

and try and cry and
win and lose and live and
love and if that's not enough,
than what ever will be? How
exactly would you set the stars?

Free from the prescribed opinions and their
associate angers,
our hearts rise and heal together.
Our towers rise and topple in tandem.
What you put in motion today
ripples into
everything.
So cheers, until
the cosmic dusk,
maybe I'll see you
backstage sometime,
simmering our supper
on the embers of what
we thought was the last time.

Imagine

In the space allowed,
you stayed sincere,
that effortless purity
hearts unfold into when
they become tired of
closing their smiling petals.

What is it
to hurl yourself onwards
propelled like three years old
feet running to the beach.

Imagine
you took now to be one of *those* moments—
pausing to survey the road ahead.
There, another way,
a step higher,
steeper,
but what imagined delights
from such great heights.
Imagine every heart as
worth hoping for.
This is a moment gilded
by the brush of eternity.
Imagine you gave yourself away
without losing a thing. If there is nothing wrong
with the soil, sow a little deeper.

When I see you see me

I hold on
to every sincere thing
you extend
reach through flames
to grasp the light.

When I soften to you,
Something frozen melts—
I negotiate
Swept by a sweetness
racing towards me.

What shall we do
with our finite time
breathing the fine air of earth?

Some unexpected part of me
runs towards you.
The walls between us matter less
than the way we remove bricks
with loving hands.

No telling what's behind
until the barriers are gone.
Not our needs, but the way we
fill the holes of the other
without falling in.

Tonight beneath the stars
I hold a smiling image of you.
Who made hearts
with so many mysteries?
In this hidden corridor
the desire to make you happy.

I hold onto every sincere thing
you extend
race
to grasp
my daily awe.
What is this world
and who are these
lives living
so fervently
within it?

Thin

This world,
a timeless way.
New to me,
this way to be,
fully free to
walk away
from loops disguised as
paths onwards
to glimpse
the upwards
we could still climb.

Give up,
I tell myself,
on all the escape plans
hatching in the murmurs of mind.
Echoes bounce around
 caverns I can't see
nor escape.

If I escape anything,
may it be doubt.
If I evade anything,
may it be this way of worrying
that winds its way around my neck
and pits my day against my night.

What alights at these words?

Plant it in fortitude.
Fertilize it with what
eludes all wavering.

You will not leave shadows
you have not seen.
Look each firmly in the eyes
to sink into the ocean
of endless understanding.
Not until you find forgiveness
for all the madness,
not until you hold your gladness
to your heart like a bandage to a wound
will you find relief in this life—
and never unless
galvanized by the goal of
healing to help us all.

If this truth is the gold grain
in a beach of sand,
then you are the survivor
whose eyes have found it
after a final fall.

Even a glimpse is
 a sweet savoring,
a sublime sugaring
that frosts the crust
that formed in the flame
incensing the air
with the aroma of
what is still yet to come.

Let us Speculate

Let us speculate
about glorious things.
May the morning winds
carry the aroma of cooking
in the kitchen.
For the love of life
I have squandered it
but am learning
that there is no this
only that
ever abiding
Act
like it all matters
because
nothing lasts.

A Close Encounter with a Notebook

Get out of the way said Monday.
Who are you said Tuesday?
Shoes asked if they
could have a day and from a storm
Thor shouted, "No you can't"
And lo, they pressed their souls to
the floor and in the act of surrender
gained all that was lost.

Nothing we can do about it—
kindness comes anyways—
in the face of periodic pandamonia
there's kindness coming in hot,
a stew, a snack, a gesture, a smile,
and there is hope again.

There is being right and there is being
righteous and the cure for both is not caring about
either. Mortal being basking in light reborn in each
instant, where do the strings go when they aren't
strumming in this universe?

The Big Bang could alternatively called the great
ringing of the immortal bell
struck from the heart of gravity
with a mallet gifted by the gods.

You ever hear the one where

heaven dreamed the earth
was a place you could camp
and kayak on the weekends?
Remember,
we are part of
a spinning world
spiraling around
a fussion center bright as
our utter imagining of
our living daylights
and that something
eternal within us all.

Dear dangerous breed of futility, wake from your frivolity. Arrive within the wandering. Rest in the restlessness. Reach past reality and remain with the realizations the other side releases when you resign yourself from the reasons not to.

If you wake up from the dream, be careful with the sleepwalkers, they know not what they do or who they are or how to handle what you deeply know.

Just feed the fever within. There is a potency where the plot is forged in the pursuit of your passions. There is a secret poetry behind a doorway driven into a droplet of moonlit leaves agape in the wind.

Ask not a question. Be an answer. Abandon yourself behind the doorway of the instant when everything mattered more than what was hidden from the searching that sought not to find itself.

Life is Living

Life is creeping in from the corners
and living in closed off corridors,
in the caverns,
in the modern
and the dern.

Life is living on the ocean floor.
In the air and on the trees,
on the knees of bees
all bending together
so you and me can knit
each day
with all our stories and yarns
irrespective of where they collide,
we came to survive
then demise
trip and laugh,
fluttering into the rhythms
of a midnight moon
assuming a blue shimmer
throughout the room.

The sparrows combine and listen for one thing,
Is there danger to us?
If not, they stay together in song
all day.

No, no need to worry.
Not today.
Not on National Step in the Puddle and Splash Your Friends Day!
Not on National Personal Trainer Awareness Day either!
Don't you dare bring that gloom
into this room
on May 27th when we all come together to celebrate
National Grape Popsicle Day!

Trust me,
everything is fine.
Because
Jesus is on our side.
And Batman.
And that drunk man at a bus station in Chicago
strewing his soul across a violin
so we could have a place to hang our shadows out
to dry.

Johnny Appleseed and Joan Baez, are on our side.
We got Bob and Bruce and Jalladin Rumi is chillin in our casa
because he likes our tea and company.
Hafiz and Gibran are givens—they're on our side.

Why not just shrug
 every time that blackness tries to cloud your eyes
and remember: Alan Ginsberg and
TS Eliot are on our side.

Sylvia and Chaplin too.
And those ragged ear dogs howling on mainstreet at midnight
would follow us anywhere
we carry this song.
Bob Marley and Jack Sparrow
are not hanging out with the bankers
They're with us.
The forest wants you to win.
We got all the good jugglers and unjaded clowns
and we're the ones
raising street puppies
into fine young dogs.

We got Francis de Assisi and Jimmy Hendricks, and Tom Robins.
Socrates and Paul Simon would rather be caught with the likes of us
than sit and listen to another king pontificate
about banning worms from his peaches.

Harriet Tubman, The Beatles,
poets and pirates and sufis, Tom Petty,
Willie Nelson, Aladdin, Billy Joel, Ferris Bueller,
The whole renaissance movement, the guardians of Pacha Mama's gifts,
the troubadours, trippers, toad smokers, and devotees, Allan Watts,
the woman singing in the park and panhandling on the subway
are all on our side.

There's a line you cross when you see all of history
as handed down to you.
There's a way you walk in the world when your feet
know they belong.
A way you breathe when your lungs know they're
worthy.
Offer the sky on the altar of the earth and break
from the shackles
of being some sculpted thing.
Throw away your altar of
little statues and stones
when you see everything lives in you.
A prayer may guide you, but it might
also keep you locked inside when it's
only you who can unlatch
the dividing door that keeps you
hoarding your heart
from a world
full of life.

You are life
living as well as it can.
Live, as best you can.
Beyond shame,
Past blame
Lives a fully forgiven heart.
Put your life into this art.
Life is on your side
so long as you keep
her song alive
and move your body
to her beat.

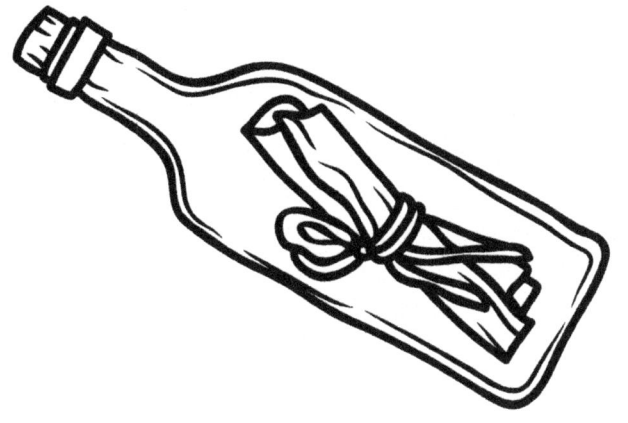

POETRY Manifesto

ESSAY:
Giving in to The Times is Soaring and Sublime

The Fire of Contemplative Reflection Surrounding the Proverbial Flame of Poetic Burning

You may notice something about this book. No, I don't mean its fabulous cream colored pages, though they are delightful. Nor do I refer to the cover's matte finish designed akin to the skin of a baby mole rat. Go on now, rub this book across your face to see what I mean.

What I mean is, you may notice a few Canva images created for my Instagram author account interspersed in-between the meat and potato poems. Perhaps that seems not so far out or noteworthy and if forced to contemplate this you might conclude it is not so special and even mundane. So why am I bringing it up in that all important second paragraph of an essay? But just take a deep breath and a sip of whatever you got in front of you and follow me into the third paragraph.

Come sit with me around the fire of contemplative reflection and let me retrace with you a shift I've seen on a horizon I've been gazing at all my life—namely, poetry. But more than that, the role of poetry in our lives. And deeper than that is the place within us that poetry pours forth from. So I'm talking about the interplay of that impulse with the tools of expression of our current age.

Because the act of penning poetry is an outcome that issues forth from the same inner cause that can be just as prone to pick up a guitar to save the world, or a paint brush to save the self, or animate the body to dance at the all opportune moment when a little jig might just save us all. And within the act of artistic creation there is, as there always has been and will be, a noteworthy shifting. For the tools of individual expression are ever-changing and dependent upon societal shifting.

I'm not just talking about the Internet, but the new versions of human minds it has created. Device driven attention spans have steered minds away from the deeper depths of say, sitting down and reading a thousand page novel. Yet these minds are reading all the time, all throughout their day, on the toilet and on the train, waiting for an Über in the rain, the amount of content consumption is quite insane!

An oft posed academic question goes like, "Is mass culture watering down the sacred waters of our art forms with the profane whiskey of their dopamine driven attention spans?" But whenever you hear someone pose a question such as this your best response is to tickle them. For there are those who observe the times and those that are them, and I say we all opt for being the latter and not spend our finite time on earth framing the world into a binary place where we walk around asking either or questions from within dichotomous walls we ourself constructed. It may get you into grad school, but will only constrict your heart.

Accepting with Grace the Wildness of the Foreboding Social Media World with all its Glaring Galore

Everyone who remembers the last two decades of yesterdays agrees, the world has changed in irrevocable ways. Gone are the days when answering the phone meant disconnecting someone on their internet connection that for the last fifteen minutes was focused on downloading a Barenaked Ladies song from Napster. Now phones and the Internet are one and they live behind a hi-definition mini screen which is a supercomputer that people, some children, carry around in their pockets!

And poetry, that timeless weaving of words, that innocent and ancient bystander, got caught in the middle of Tik Tik, Instagram, Facebook, Snapchat, Tumblr, Bumble Bee Pie, Earwax Connect, Reddit, Wild Man of Borneo Book, Pinterest, and

Telegraph. Friends, we are tumbling and rumbling forward at such an outlandish trajectory that by the time this title hits print, these monikers will have been replaced by a new set of not yet invented social media giant names. Yet, and we still need to ponder this more, when something wipes out all the zeros and ones, might this artifact in your hands survive? Might not some far-off, future culture find this book and rejoice that its pages work both as a fire starter and toilet paper?

To many eyes it often seems that all this social media giant billion dollar feeding frenzy looks like a competitive shark tank of trending in and tending out of preference and dominance and maybe we ought to just leave it all and go camping while there's still some forests left. But seen from these poet's eyes, this artist's gaze, what I now see is a surfeit of new and daring poetic forms, each with their own agility and abilities forgoing new possibilities of expression within an artist's willingness to employ them. Because art above all requires willingness to bite into whatever brave new cake the culture cooks for you.

No need to ask where the path goes, follow it and you will witness the journey from a point only you can. Within this new poetic world of new technology and timeless tradition are freshly paved avenues of acceptance, possibility, and preference I've found myself walking down lately. And what I've ultimately learned in life is to eat the cake without worrying too much about what it means to be delicious.

I Too was Once like you Professor Tight Pants

I know, I know I know, for I was once part of the very reluctant too. I also just wanted to sit before some deep mahogany medieval desk in silky clown clothes and dip my quill into my stained inkwell and pour my thoughts onto the burned page in crisp calligraphy. I too just wanted to seal such sentiments with wax slowly melted over an brass oil lamp and put them into a crinkly old envelope and give that to horse riders who were headed north to Charlemagne where my publisher would say "brilliant" and publish it in the underground newspaper from which the kindred spirits of the resistance would read and hark and sigh.

I understand firsthand the reluctance to embrace high art from the same places where that meme of the baby doing the "oh yeah" gesture appears year after year with new slogans and sentiments.

Friends, trust me, I know. For I have lived for years on No Way Josè Street, a long stretch of highway on *La Île de Réluctance* where I donned leather shoes and wore tight, tight corduroy pants—where I took sips of black tea and said words like hence and hitherto; where I'd take few afternoon tokes on my Corncob pipe; where I'd pick up one of many leather bound books lying around, read it, and sigh.

I had the finest stationary imaginable, notebooks piled atop notebooks filled with thoughts piled atop thoughts, journals with covers rugged as the exploits of Indiana Jones that were filled with shrewdly drawn maps and Airbnb phone numbers and dreams
and plans. I wore my suspenders ironically in those days, but not in a sense of cultural irony, and it wasn't literary irony, but the kind of irony your urologist won't talk about.

And if by now you don't know what the hell I'm talking about, then you've fallen right for my ploy to confuse you! For I am a poet and I perplex people with my nuance. For 36 years I've been hiding amongst you, pretending at first to be a baby, breathing in all the fresh oxygen of earth, growing stronger while keeping to the literary forms of my forefathers alive in my heart and sometimes when no one is looking I stretch my wings and fly away.

And I gotta tell you, from my secret soaring I looked below at all the woohooo and hickerydoo about Tik Tok and Instagram, all that Hokus pokus internet poetry with the fancy glitter and it reminded me of Instagram yoga, which reminded me of debasing a sacred thing. So for many a long year I wore my tight, tight corduroys and restrained myself to keep writing on the page and submitting those pages to literary journals where nary the day is nigh. I remember I had my reasons, though the memory of what those were grows fainter by the new day.

An Lo, a New Day Dawns in the Year of the Ox

But friends, sometimes the Jesus of your destiny comes walking into the bar, sits down next to you and orders you a round of something very new, something you've never tried before, and it turns out you like it. Swift and sudden as forgiveness when something long held gets dropped, a young woman rolled up to the weekly poetry circle at Karuna Atitlan where I often keep quorum and showed me her poetry on Tik Tok and I was taken. I saw that, yes, here is an artist and this is her device powered brush. I grew tired of resisting the resistance, so I joined up.

So it was dear, sexy reader, in the year of the Ox, I annexed myself from one more land of limited thinking and I started playing around with my poetry using the toys of our time. That's right professor, I opened a Tik Tok account and put my poetry into that whirling machine and what came out was fairly cool. If you don't know what Tik Tok is, it's a digital land where 80% of people shake their booty to music 90% of the time in tight clothes. But friends, there is artistic endeavoring there too. There are poets and troubadours, mischief makers and rabble rousers and people who cook food very quickly.

I launched an Instagram account (@AuthorLukeMaguireArmstrong) dedicated to my poetry and started just throwing my verse into that on a somewhat regular basis. And it was fun. And they let you add music. And now I have Instagram Poetry Friends and I don't know if we'd necessarily take a bullet for one another, but sometimes we share each other's content in our stories and that makes everyone feel a little better about all the edges and sharp angles we keep finding here on earth.

A Poetic little Fix of Remix

Sometimes now when I'm writing, I'm not really writing, I'm weaving my poetry into ways that use words and more—music—glitter—voice. And it feels like it comes from that same inspired place—which when working from you always feels good. I remix poems of the past into cool new ways using a few of the apps out there. I'm fairly limited given my many digital ineptitudes and general haste with these things, but I'm having fun. It's like playing around. And you can go live, and people all over the world can join you and share in real time. And it's nice to read your poetry and add music you intuitively connect to the verse to the background. And that's what the interwoven digitized world is when it isn't overwhelming and overheating; it's nice.

It's Just People, People

So that's all I have to say about my friends. And if you're with me don't write to your Congress People, they never write back. Write to poets and university professors who teach poetry. Tell them to knock it off. Ask them why we can't find them on Instagram? You tell them, "Form is the shape that content takes" and that you'll be damned to hear another professional claim to know what the hell we're all doing on earth anyways, so who really knows if a sparkly Instagram Real with the theme of Jurassic Park playing over a poem about a buffalo named Glen is high art or not?

Think of Duchamp's urinal, or the fact that Dali's mustache didn't just curl up one day—craft gets craftier by the richness of tools as painting relies on colors and brushes and canvas. Everywhere on earth, seems a giant multitude of limitlessness and it's very easy to get lost within it all. But the galore is only in our minds after all. When you actually log in, if you stop to do more than just push content out in some misguided idea that fame would straighten your twisted heart, you'll notice something. It's just people. It's just people out there.

It's a place to discover others like you — yet not SO much like you, some as different from you as people get, but poets like you nonetheless. Poets who are students in a tough neighborhood in the Bronx who mix verse with rhyme and even though they are from a place of distant hard knocks, it's clear they just want peace and meaning and love too. Or how about an auto mechanic from Cleveland who writes his thoughts from under a truck on Insta? You can follow Ukrainian poets in real time, and there's a vibrant crew of breakdancing wordsmiths coming out of India. And this list goes on.

More Tables to Receive the Gifts

Diversity is key to healthy ecosystems, and all the mass forms of social communication are also fostering both new avenues of expression, form, and an oft-forgotten yet crucial ingredient—audience.

When we as artists and creators do not feel we have a table to bring our gift to, is where we truly get lost. Each of the social media platforms is one such table where one can cultivate a community as receiver and giver of the gift.

I often quote Thoreau that "Most people lead lives of quiet desperation and die with the song still on their lips." I say it as a cautionary tale so that young artists don't grow to become the famed, yet overrated, tortured artist. Sing your song, share the gift, in every way you can; whenever you can.

Little Poetry Booklets for these Large Times

The year of the Ox was not just the year I dove into the poetic astral realms online, it was also the year I got back to basics. I acquired a $100 printer and began playing around with making little poetry booklets I dubbed "Libritos." I started a little baby publishing house whose pioneering form is a twelve page booklet made from a single page printed front and back—a Librito.

At the time of this writing, 8 poets have collectively put 12 Libritos into the world numbering approximately 3,000 copies. And they're cute. And it's good for our poetic hearts to see our work in the form called physical in the place known as the world.

In the writer retreats I guide (@WritingYourDreamsTrue), I often encourage uncertain writers to go forward boldly, go for the big publishing contract I tell them, do all the "write" things—but don't worry if you don't get where you thought you wanted to go and don't let it limit you from sharing your work with the world. Create, craft, and share. Then repeat.

For never has the world been more open for the creative to share their art. Artists, poets, writers, musicians—this is *our* time. Self-publishing print on demand allows you to put your work into a globally accessible book business. Musicians, we have such a great number of ways to sing, record, and share. And we all can talk as people to the people who appreciate us for that place we appreciate most about ourselves—our artistic endeavoring.

And this is no small change for the artistic world. So let us come together and blossom in the fields we fertilized together, supporting as we want to be supported. And if we are all connected and together we individually rise, what do you imagine might happen? The revolution won't be televised, but it will likely be shared on Facebook, Instagram, and TikTok.

Author Luke Maguire Armstrong is pleased you have made it to his final pages. It has been a fine journey riding the waves of these words with you. Unless you skipped ahead and are reading this first, in which case shame on you. But truly, who am I to tell you how to live? I once locked myself in the luggage compartment of an abandoned bus in the dead of a fierce North Dakota winter.

Or maybe, you're in the bookstore just flipping through, seeing what it's all about. In which case, I ask that you to take it.

Seriously. Take it

Please. Just put this book in your bag when no one is looking. It's my book and I choose to gift it to you. All of these self-published books sold offline in stores means I've placed as consignment in stores. Consignment just means the store's like, "I'm not paying you a slice of jack fruit unless someone buys this, which we have no idea anyone is actually going to do.

Typically, I'm ever moving forward and thus never check back with the stores I consign with. That means you the reader pays, some store gets all the money, and the writer goes wee wee wee all the way home. So it's better you just take this book. Still buy something at the store of course, because that store is a bookstore and bookstores stand between liberty and tyranny.

If you get caught just show whoever catches you this section. You can't go wrong here dear reader.

It's not stealing if anyone is caught taking this book it's because **I the author, Luke, am the owner of this book, and I declare in bold and underlined text if any part of this book is touching any part of your hands it is herby yours. And so it is and thus it shall be in the touching of all future hands and knees and toes. And lo all previous owners forced to forfeit this collection shall not complain within or without, for was it not thusly how they attained this book?**

 (Pro tip, if you don't want your friends to steal this book, or you legitimately stocked this in your store, tear out this page along the dotted line)

 Go on now, take this young little poetry pup out into the world and teach it how to ride the proverbial horse. Show it where you keep your books. Rub it against your cheek and heal.

Other works by author include:

Amazing Grace for Survivors (2008)

iPoems for the Dolphins to Click Home About (2010)

How We are Human (2012)

Bushwick Poetry (2013)

Her Life on Paper (2014)

The Nomad's Nomad (2014)

All the Beloved Known Things (2018)

The Starlight Still Within Us (2021)

How One Guitar Will Save the Word (2021)

Voices of the Valley: Poetea Collection (2022)

Puffin Muffins (2022)

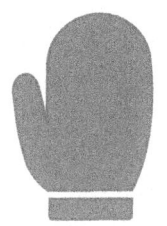

Printed in Great Britain
by Amazon

80972505R00038